THE RECLUSIVE SOLDIER

A POETRY CONCEPT ALBUM ON MENTAL HEALTH

ABHIJIT SHANKARAN

Copyright © Abhijit Shankaran
All Rights Reserved.

This book has been self-published with all reasonable efforts taken to make the material error-free by the author. No part of this book shall be used, reproduced in any manner whatsoever without written permission from the author, except in the case of brief quotations embodied in critical articles and reviews.

The Author of this book is solely responsible and liable for its content including but not limited to the views, representations, descriptions, statements, information, opinions and references ["Content"]. The Content of this book shall not constitute or be construed or deemed to reflect the opinion or expression of the Publisher or Editor. Neither the Publisher nor Editor endorse or approve the Content of this book or guarantee the reliability, accuracy or completeness of the Content published herein and do not make any representations or warranties of any kind, express or implied, including but not limited to the implied warranties of merchantability, fitness for a particular purpose. The Publisher and Editor shall not be liable whatsoever for any errors, omissions, whether such errors or omissions result from negligence, accident, or any other cause or claims for loss or damages of any kind, including without limitation, indirect or consequential loss or damage arising out of use, inability to use, or about the reliability, accuracy or sufficiency of the information contained in this book.

Made with ♥ on the Notion Press Platform
www.notionpress.com

Contents

Contents

Preface

Reality can be a convoluted vortex that refuses to traverse in a straight line. We humans as a species are consciously programmed to believe that light immediately follows the dark tunnel. Assuming that to be true, the poems ahead will take you through the stark realities of this dark tunnel in the hope of attaining the light ahead.

Centralized on my perception and experiences of and with reality, depression and empowerment I take you through my journey thus far. I leave it to the perception of you wonderful and insightful readers with the hope that you will both enjoy the read and be uplifted.

I have written rather deeply about the sensitive workings of my mind fighting through the difficulties of reality. By writing on several sensitive topics I not only look the devil in the eye but also encourage others to listen to their inner voice. In the good intention of speaking my truth, I hope I encourage my readers to also search for their inner voice.

A voice that is pure, innocent, intuitive and insightful.

Acknowledgements

The poems express the contemplation, suffering and learnings I have been through to give a voice to those who aren't able to or are trying to. I thank god for giving me the courage to attempt to turn pain into lessons and try to serve mankind via compassion & humility. Externalizing one's inner demons in a manner that is cathartic, therapeutic and uplifting takes a lot of courage. I thank myself for gathering the courage to do so through this book.

My friend, Sukriti, I thank you for designing the book cover. It wouldn't be possible for anyone else to have done justice to my thoughts the way you have through this artwork. Thank for you listening to my pain, suffering, happiness and joy through and through all these years. For this and further books to come, you continue to be a wonderful support system.

My brother, Prasana, I wouldn't be able to put pen on paper if not for you. I find thanking you in itself to be inadequate because words fail to express my gratitude to you.

I thank Notion Press Publishing for providing a wonderful platform for the book to be published. Here's hoping for a continued journey of creativity and excellence.

1. Displaced

'**Displaced**' introduces readers to the inner turmoil one goes through. It specifically sheds light on the conflict between what is conventionally called the 'Mind' and the 'Heart'. The polarizing effects of conditioning (societal, parental, biological etc) wedge one between flying with freedom. Often one is like a bird flapping their wings but within the confines of a cage.

2 Boxes

Let me take you through a journey
A journey through your mind
2 emanating sources of energy
Neurons puzzled and petrified

Your world emanates from these boxes
One who you are, one who you're told to be
The crossfire leaves you blinded
A simmering voice quickly subsided

A lifespan spent on searching
A voice, its sound unheard
For the world dictates what we hear
'Run quicker', 'Keep up', 'Push harder'
For whom? For what? Why bother?

Presumptions, assumptions galore
Pretentiousness seeps through the floor
A lifespan spent on searching
A voice, its sound unheard

A loop well-circuited disguised
Trapped toxic the devil's surprise

Springs out of the box with satire
It laughs, we're mocked, flash fire

The box that we are in quickly rushes
To fight the dark voices, those liars
That trick us, that break us, soul crushers
And just when you think it is over?
With more camps and retreats, they surge harder

And inside one's head, one is screaming
For the pain, one would rather be killed
Like doomed to be sparks, holy voices
Still resonate, smiling, still hoping
By this time the light quickly fades
Overwhelmed by the power of the dark
A lifespan spent on searching
A voice, its sound unheard

Black or White

You can't have it both ways
He said over the phone
If only he could convince himself of the same
That hope from the masquerader is hopeless helplessness

Does one blame oneself for continued belief in the charlatan?
Does one heap a pile of misery on themselves for being blind?
Does one raid the emptiness within with unperturbed shallowness?
Does one face the hot breeze of undeterred stubbornness?

Finish what you started and don't half-track
He said over the phone
If only he could convince himself of the same
That grief from the perpetrator is rewound and repeated

He put his phone down and gasped for breath
He knew he'd be there soon and would require her aid
The artillery support fights a dizzy haze
The gentle touch to a fainting mind
He reaches for a knife He reaches to the railing
He teaches himself to hide
He teaches he is better off in his grief

As he fights his mind every day

The heights of clouded misogyny
The weight of unguided irony
The nauseating paranoia of underpar existence

He takes god's name
As he asks for forgiveness
As he asks for hopefulness

The atheist who always hoped for a higher power
The atheist couldn't be angry and not believe in him
Now he stands in the middle of nowhere
He hopes the grass is greener eventually

Yet substantially circumnavigated
Yet strangely uninhibited
As he now knows the battle is not with his mind

It is with the blinding alley masquerading the innocent
The battery downed his inspiration
That death had more certainty
his eyes lied to him

He believed every word

Conviction and contentment

He reaped every effort
Convicted and convoluted

He chooses to be the man in the mirror
She is worried he will walk away from it
He fights for as long as he can

She captures every moment knowing it may be over
The arc that saved millions
May have bred the wrong race
The cold sweat trickling down his chin
He wakes up from his nightmare
He had much rather fallen back asleep

For the eyes he sees he doesn't believe
For the tree has been subjected and judged
Its leaves slowly start to wither
Its lips slowly start to turn blue

Then a surging instinct to live troubleshoot
Then a thunderous applause awakened the curfew
The rising tide above the fading moon
The werewolf bares its wrath underscoring

Unwinding and intent-filled
He channels his energy again

He tries knowing he goes nowhere
He does it for somebody

For as long as it can save him from a dire consequence

Of acting on impulse or justifiable backtracking

He picks up the phone one last time

It gives him hope somehow to hold on for another day

He humours the devil by massaging his pain

As the demon laughs and says he will be back again

July

That beautiful smile that roared with its angelic voice
That screamed at the demon and soothed the wounded
That empowered the trying and uplifted the defeated

You didn't succumb to the demon
You bid adieu to the pain
That wrenched you for the longest
That drenches me forever

That outspoken confrontation with tear-filled sorrow
The voice ranged across a roller coaster of emotions
That embraced the darkness with might
That embarked on a quest towards happiness
Your legacy speaks for itself
The tyranny is finally over

With you gone how will I fight for 20 more years
A soldier gone but never defeated
I wished I hadn't woken up the day you left
I wished I hadn't seen half of you the day before

You are here with me still echoing through
You fought the closing walls with me when I couldn't
I still can't, please revert, return and save me

Those who cared never really did
Those who believed have given up

I knew from far your smile hid your anguish
Extinguished, and exhausted I lie huddled

I look into your eyes searching for a possibility
With tears rolling I still laugh at your wit

Bittersweet, I know there isn't a way to restart

Who would have thought
Who would have believed
Please listen to my screaming
It may not be as angelic as yours

We do share the choices we made
For better or worse we stood by them
We fought our minds as it tore us apart
We fought our past for a future that may never last
The supernova orbiting my thoughts

Your voice is the only soothing symphony
A strangely innate emotion I subscribe to
A nagging narcissism that I fight every moment
The devil's crimson strut across his eyes

The devil's silence louder than his shrapnel's

I try to do what you always did
To face the demon to fight the impulse
If I knew I could join you after the finale
I knew you would send me to war to battle again

Event Horizon

The lesser said the better
Perhaps the most gravely misinterpreted philosophy
The closer I came to an understanding
The farther from closure I drifted

The side of you I never thought existed
Hot and cold I felt neglected
I opened my heart and instantly regretted
The farther from closure I drifted

Does it take skills to care?
Or is wrath, the devil's ace card?
Is shattering how we fix things?
Or is ego the devil's poker face?

Seeking for that singularity within you
I swam past tidal waves giving myself to you
In hope to be one with you
Not to out you, not to outrun you

Tired of being an emotional punching bag
Tired of being neglected
I opened my heart, and instantly regretted

The farther from closure I drifted

The masquerading you never needed to
Did I not sell my soul to you?
Be compared and yelled I still embraced the side you showed
Did I not deserve to see past the event horizon?

Was I a compromise amidst all the comparisons?
Was I a disappointment to your expectations?

Seeking oneness I lost sight of my singularity
People don't change they grow said a friend
Singularity I realized was not the journey nor the end
It all comes from you, it is all you are I realized

Was I a little too late contemplating how to die?
As ego slapped love on its face
The devil smirked at my helplessness

I let you go for love was not my fault
I let you go for the pain was relentless
Inches from death and gasping for breath,
I decided to let you go

All the while,

I opened my heart and instantly regretted

The farther from closure I drifted

Lost Key

If the mind made peace with the heart
I wonder if there would be fewer conflicts
Pain would still exist
But perhaps suffering may come to an end

For simplicity so esoteric
For happiness unbound
While the truth remains a confidant
The memories become a scavenger hunt

As one subsides a newer reason
The words once said scar a burn
What heals remain sealed
No more a word
No more a weep
Afraid to rekindle lost faith
Tried, Tested, Unrewarded

As the stars fight through the burdened sky
Spreading their glitter across
Like broken wings they fall
Glistening less; Twitching more
From being loved to loving all

To holding pain and numbing love

As the eyes meet, dark magic springs
Digging through what is not
Sharp & lustrous over deadwood
Forgive what's dead to forget the past

But the dead though buried come screaming through
worse than a ghost these memories haunt you
God's words a far lost echo
The voice within you lost and forgotten

2. The Crossfire

*'**The Crossfire**' digs deeper into the war between conflicting ideas, identities, feelings and beliefs. The battlefield is so intense, that nobody knows who sides with whom. As echoing voices scream across one another, ammunitions of curses and accusations bleed painful emotions, anxiety, lowness and desperation.*

1. *Who is it that is caught in the crossfire?*
2. *On whose behalf is the battle happening?*

In your Heart

A noble disguise concealed evidence
Cold breath warming
Void filled essence
Eyes cut to infinity

Brought back by the enemy
Trained to mask the mask
Dried leaves and stones
But a single tear

Floods your bones
Warm blood a need
Creating your creed
Putting yourself below

With a smile adding to the sorrow
Disconnected to connect
To an unnecessary need
A need of want and not greed

You sing through somehow
With a broken wing
Nightmares to befriend

That's how days begin

In your heart

Yet inside buried
Is the missing wing
Hoping to stick on
Hoping to take off

Cold feet sweating
Lost a sense of seeing
Everything seems dark
Everything cold between

Yet inside buried
Is the search for joy
Running down the stairways
Or dancing through the top

Living by your dreams
Entrusting the loved
You hold onto that piece

That kickstarts your life
And when you find that wing

Let me know

I'll be there to watch you go
To see you contented inside
And soar so high

To see you touch the skies
To see you so happy
To see you so alive

Dancing and singing
A humble thunder
Striking energy
Giving life
Giving joy

In your heart

If Only Lies Could Tell The Truth
If Only The Past Couldn't Foretell
A forfeit wouldn't forget

The sunrise wouldn't lighten
The sunset wouldn't set
Packed in a chamber

Into the wild
Breathing vacuum
The bloodstreams die

Fevers scaling higher than ever
The mind lost control and the words don't fear
The rotten rips and the voices clear

Questions

You mercilessly beat my thoughts
With daggers rowing through the dark
How do I go through all this pain?

Weighed down by guilt
Blood lost wings gained
Some shadows bloom into the light

And Out of danger into sight
Fighting through a troubling night
Why isn't my end or start so bright

One finds himself in locks and ties
But finds his way through keys and lies
Pretending all those memories

Meant nothing for ones need for life
And crying through this blinding ride
See heartbeats racing an ocean ride

Rise high above and fall below
Like a mirror that lies
In a scattered glow

Your questions make your reasons worse
Laid down smothered by a smiling curse
That writes your future in your hands

And burns down faith like water on sand
The anger builds and danger grows
you clothe your wrong
The cold stains glow

So whilst one cries himself to sleep
you hide your way to a fame filled treat

Hope luck brings glory and reason smile and
bring more peace to a wordless crime and
questions answered right in time
to save your world, that kid in mind

Declaration

When you run out of words to explain
When you run out of ideas to ascertain

A situation at hand slipping away
A dagger smashed through your vein

As the rivers bleed pure
Fighting for their innocence

Guilty of nothing and no cure?
seeking some way to bring down this pain

Falling and fading out is a destination
Forgetting and reassessing a devastation

Ignorance is a prerogative of the selfish
Because the word genuine is overrated

Feeding answers to a mountain of questions
Seeping through the sand is a cowardly redemption

While reasons explain a terrific situation
The heart blows and the end is a declaration.

Domino Effect

Accountability as massaged through a social contract
Supreme power accentuated through one's prowess

Fundamentally flawed and emotionally misconstrued
A spiteful act on the neatly assembled crockery
A bull whip effect on the less fortunate

Powerplay's and games newly compounded
Monopolies and monuments established
To one's self-attribution

Where the deserved are stripped
Where the deserved are destroyed

A symphony arising through a silhouette promise
A tangled regiment through a bottomless cup

That must begin from somewhere
That must begin from someone

But accountability is power with subjugation
Where motives matter and actions more
When both lie where does one go

What value one seeks in what lies ahead

The mountains melted quicker

The snow skewed smoulder

Extra Mile

As your life flashes before your eyes
While the ones you hurt try saving your life
The pulse within a heartbeat away

The screaming inward to silence the mystery
What you deserve and what you don't

One's free will is underrated
One's thoughts were curated
One will never see the light of day

The polished sound of the crackling symphony
The satisfaction that comes from wrecking misery
The itch and cure to one's tear-filled eye sockets

No references, attributes no one to care enough
While swirled across the floor the chilling wood

The smoke-filled horror catalysing ooze
A crimson dark emotional breakdown
That seeps through your skin and into your heart

Does one care to care enough?

To further their dirt and clear the dirt?
To bleed a void a love filled spur

The angels sympathetic, the voices unheard
Does one care to care enough?

To meet one's eye and accept for one
To fight the fight that fights inward
The battle the lost that lost toward

To emote and empower
To prosper and endeavour

3. Annihilation

*'**Annihilation**' takes readers through a crucial turning point in the journey. There is a willingness to dig within and explore the unfamiliar. In doing so, there is a seeming annihilation of oneself, and in that annihilation, there is a rising of a phoenix bird waiting to transcend the limitations set by the cage it is in.*

The Dig

Searching within the black hole of uncertainty
Somewhere lies a journey not too deep

Perhaps midway through this divide trenches from below
Where the lights go dim and the dig reverse
Suffocating in the chilling niceness

That embraces the near dead and near confounded
The despairing hopelessness of staying alive
A dig too deep too far behind

The meaning to life is the empty vessel
Where solitude basks amidst the shallowness

Where gratitude bakes amongst the emptiness
The wreckage float through your savageness

A landscape painted with protruding clips
Of chewed off nails from sweating drifts
The heartbreak gasps for a breath of hope

Too weak to clasp the surging purge
How far more down this black hole
How far more towards nothingness

The opposite of hope a seeming hopelessness

The farfetched outreach to a summer's complacence
The dewdrops breathe life
The teardrops gleam love

You sit with me in this dark trench
You sit until the last spark of the lighter
A shallow and humorous conversation
A bittersweet twist to a miserable life

You find hope innate
The cataclysm within me
You give me something to work with
Or perhaps when I die my last memory

Unfamiliarity

I look into your eyes
As my feet touch the railing 10 feet up
The 5 seconds of control may never be
Your hand extended pulling me to certainty

Perhaps lost in the sound of your concern
Is my heart for a moment as I am pain-free
I suppose until the painkillers wear off
Unless you stay forever with me

The quest to find the truth
The meaning and purpose of life
The urge to fight the hypocrisy

That demolishes mankind
That destroyed my lifeboat
Or possibly east of my room across the window

The sun glares through except the pane
I hide behind the pain hoping the rays deflect
But now I shut the curtain extinguishing the heat

The heat doesn't cease to exist

The dead don't come back to life
The future to power was an illusion

A dissolved past so consuming
The walls close in like quicksand
The straight-faced heartlessness

The cold-blooded mercilessness
A roller-coaster of emotions fills the cup
Happiness is not one of them

For ecstasy has been the opposite of pain
For success has been the opposite of failure
Stuck between closing doors

Those that were shut, to begin with
A scarf gripped too weak to strangle through
As blood oozes past the fading morphine

Far Away from me perhaps never to be seen
The worried face straps my hand firmly
The puppet master and the hand of god

You have your vulnerability
You have your struggle

And yet my sweating palms have company
Perhaps a validation I never received
For the first time in a while more than a painkiller

A silhouette so picturesque
gives me light in the darkness

Love in War

For the first time,
no answers in my pocket
I seek serenity
only to lose my dignity

That angel voice I search for
only screams I hear around
if only a smile could wipe those tears
if only a shoulder could carry my fears

All the dust and black smoke
All the bullets and dead souls
and I'm scared of stepping a stone
what if I'm found; ripped and thrown?

The sound screeching through my ears
deafening my bleeding soul
I see that boy hiding under the litter
I pray the snakes spare their slither

From the leftovers, we try to build
what could be a remnant of the future
Hoping not to replicate the gaze

A race that is never to fulfil

When war breaks they say hope follows
if there is night there is day they say

Perhaps a solitude so ghastly I pray
For the past delusion holds the only way

We hold each other
To save light; add wood
let our ashes be the remains
but our souls go on forever

Left with little choice but uncertainty
Our only downfall is our redemption

Come and save what's slipping away
come to relinquish the last dew drops
for humanity, for that love so parched
Drip by drip to restart

50-50

Is it half full or half empty?
thoughts screaming through swiftly
Am I falling or rising?
Should I be laughing or crying?

Let me live in my coffin
die in my burial

Switch off to tune in
Break off to break in
Die inside to show life
So you live and I survive
Love takes its form
Like water in a cup

While your eyes say a lot
The words don't really play right

A blurry image yet crystal clear
a sorrow face my mask is clear
you can see through my sorrow
and bring me out to a tomorrow

If only I could but I can never say

I'll still wait 'cause I know some things never fade

In the memories by the images

Lives life sorrow, a name and happiness

Belief

It's not just the holding of a hand
It's the grip with which it's held

It's not the tightness and one's strength
It's the firm hold and a smile till the end

Like the burning sun, so magnanimous
or the faint twinkling of the stars
The sun melting our skin

Through sweat, the stars, still twinkling
Though so far it ain't over till it's over

Not until the last drop falls
The ten billionth drop completes

The ocean a single word can tear you apart
The touch of a million words
A belief can only make it flow

Excuses made to cover a belief
That was never too enough
That was never too deep

Belief is a believed belief
Reality comes from belief
If that omen end comes

You have the belief
To move past the very beliefs
That belief made you believe

4. Cathartic Remnants

*'**Cathartic Remnants**' is the very 'in-between' that one may call a 'no man's land'. One is neither here nor there in their healing journey and it can be terrifying. They realize that the cage while seemingly cruel is also equally comforting as a means of security. One is almost always preparing for the toxic patterns the locked cage offers, and the freedom to fly somehow while liberating is equally difficult for most because one doesn't know where the sky will take them. One in essence doesn't know what their wings can do for them. Their identification with what they are not takes them away from who they are. Freedom.*

Escapist

A god of thought
An evil warlord
A white sheet staring
And the clouds growing dark

Some place to hide
Rings chains devised
Forsaken events

The water inside dries
and a galloping
beyond mountains and creeks
and a glistening
of your evil heart and your grin

A word so fond
you race across the skies
and while your focus is diverted
all the pleadings fall off

A burning misery
a lifeboat wandering
resolutions dissipating

an arrival departing

A smothering so loved
a deep cut that reaps through
and the rooftops creak grumbling
and your heart thumping and pounding

You run away from the sight
to find a place on the outside
convinced of owning the lost

and of breathing the air you cannot
and you drown in your uncertainty
to make yourself a life;

It's not how it's supposed to be
to convince of having the lost
and of breathing the air you cannot breathe

To see yourself amongst the stars
when you know you are not one inch
to carve a place in the wild

you rename your passion your ecstasy
Or maybe that's how it is to be

A journey somewhere to interject
An objection soul-slapping

The toxicity builds up in your mind
Escaping or moving to a better place
the debate left unanswered and open to opinions
You drown in your uncertainty

Give it Away

It takes forever to build
cement conceal and live
walk away with no guilt
assuming its your filth

Sometimes you've got to survive
closed up act like you rejoice
locked up yet open wide
unopened, kept closed in a lie

You give away
what took a while
You give away
what made us smile
You give away
everything we tried
You give away
so what do I hide

When you love but it back stabs you
when a scold hurts more
than the hurt hurts you

You were lost inside
yet you found your way
to a world somewhere
where blood freezes a stay
for a reason of mine
you gave me away

You've not given up
but you've given away
Don't they cry for you?
Why did you give it away?

It's like you're cold and warm at the same time
equal yet lowered to the ground
burning up and falling to the ground

Afraid to realize
that you are at paradise
you know deep inside
you gave us away scratched
and torn it cannot heal
you just gave it away

Silent

Eyes closed and hearts racing
The truth is out and words blinding
Like the wake of the sun through the new born
The pain stings and the choking

The power of silence is unspoken
The feelings shattered; separated
A reason you find convincing
Numbs, lies, but not the bleeding

You speak to me through your eyes
And smother me with your silence
I speak to you, my soul, my life
You read past the shallowness

Pretending to smile efficiently
You convince my thoughts magically
That you will show up when I need you
But when you do?
Past the moment
Past the hurry

Mirrors Lie

When what you build is a lie
All you've known set on fire
Everyone standing tall
Bleeding nose, broken thighs

Every word risen high
Little pieces broken tiles,
Disquiet and scathing files
Left the cold wind to survive

Breathing love till words are dry
Every autumn springs with joy
Reclusive and sullen thoughts
All the love you've known is gone

The good seems undefined
One's motive redefined
Tranquil and unified
And live with private lies

The truth remains volatile
As long as it is easily concealed
It's easier to know the truth

Than accept its consequences and live with it

Still fallen down and bleeding nose
Breathing love for hope and control

But the truth is that the truth is disfigured
To clear the screen and act unchanged

The deserved lose their place
To no meaning and no face
While the won feels like the lost
And happiness a disgrace

The lies threatening
with armours and swords upright
a voice cold and hopeless
Because even mirrors have learned to lie

Secret

Like a flightless bird
The endless dawn
The desperation
A cold blooded song

A distant sound
Not too profound
Like open secrets
Tore me down

Forced into the silence
Broken down
The tumour set to burst me out
There is not much to fret about

You came right in and threw me out

Let me be alone
Don't save me
Just let me lay alone
Don't save me

A forsaken history

Don't blink with uncertainty
Just let me be
Don't come and save me
Don't regret
This secret
Just let me be
Don't come and save me

Let me be alone
Don't come and save me
Just let me lay alone
Don't come and save me

A feeling of no security
Giving up on dreaming
Disbelief and immaturity
Like broken facts lost credibility

A mask to show my true identity
The truth to cover a lie so correctly
You found a way to pierce into me
a mistake or on purpose?
a question so obsolete

A foundation you dropped so carelessly

run away before my voice tears your smile

Let me be alone

Don't come and save me

Just let me lay alone

Don't come and save me

5. Reinvented

*'**Reinvented**' is grieving the past to welcome the present. There is an unexplained solitude that arises, a release, a catharsis. Except this time, it is not from the remnants of the past but of the future that appears like a flamboyant ventriloquist. Different shapes and forms of the same past projected into the future now slowly begin to lose their veiling power. The reinvention begins with the identification of mental patterns. The reinvention exposes the reality behind this illusory power.*

Unexplained

Life begins with a certain assumption
Strong or weak gather some conviction
Like a teardrop hanging by a leaf
All hope seems dry and no retreat

With a mentor reap
And a skylight-deep
All the stars seem lost like an angel tweet

When a grip turns and crushes you down
Definitions of hard change slowly meltdown
as a back-stab curls all the hope below
as the heart sublimes and the lava blows

Far deep down a seeping soil lay instincts
burnt lay instincts dry

Follow the stars from north below and
see miseries creep and memories lie
all the meanings mean a greater good
for a life was once and the life you choose

All the sunlight masked by the elevation

of a magic strong just a revelation

with failures stripping with every step

where the cowards fall and the brave face death

Quietude

The constant battle between the past that was
and the future that isn't
We struggle, snorkel to stay afloat
As things go wrong beyond our control we retract
Pull ourselves together against adversity

The abstract ideation of a reality consumed
The darkest spaces governing our answers
When '**We**' become '**I**',
'I' becomes loneliness
The weeping heart stitches through a lonely battle
That traverses between blinding ashes

An ever so surreal certainty
In this dark alley some stay
That reminds us that the wounds caused and the wounds we
caused don't define us
That stays with us through
the biting cold of these dark spaces

Holding, breathing, comforting this gripping sorrow
The tears of blood were wiped from my eyes
the scorching repercussions of a turbulent world

a respite taken by the very demons
that seeps into my thoughts, words and beliefs
where silence hurts more than the imposing undertone

Some wipe off our tears
Swim in the darkness with us

They are our unconditional angels;
our undeterred strengths

That lets us know we are not what we are made to be defined to be
we are defined by our belief in our own beliefs

Gratitude knows no bounds, love knows no hate
I wish you all the best and a happy life ahead
While I pick myself with my angels
who guide me through the very darkness

That I thought you were in for with me
That I thought we would walk out together
I wake the inner child within me,
the untapped enthusiasm to live
I thank you for the good memories
but not the ones that intoxicated me

That sucked me into a vortex where

my angels keep frantically searching for me

As I hold back my grief and tears

until I see them

I see light

I know who I want to be

Layers

Context for one and content for the other
A blend of sorrow with aspirational figures
That drive us forward, our goals and our desires

Be stripped off the image an unscathed satire
We live in a world where toxicity brews amass
Be tipped off the boat biting cold inch deep dark

And while those that journey fill bottomless cups
Layer by layer you seek a one told desire
And in this time line expectations sprout higher

As self-doubt wreaks content
realism screams satire
Down-town smoke-filled and
wry deep down broken yet meek

as the shrapnel's bleed crimson paint skies
with your blood leaving marks of empathy
scripting off of a dreamer only
layer by layer seeking
a one told desire

Companions embark on journeys of their own
led by cold heartedness a layer there untold
I see you I feel you weak now yet heart stronger

With truth on your side you need not fear my dear
And in this lone walk you see love from within you
You build yourself stronger magnetic magnificent
And layer by layer those left revert realizing

A journey you embarked alone and unwinding
Sharp edges of glasses that pierce through emotions
Let those people in forgive, forget, keep walking

The dewdrops of wisdom inspire that desire
And moment by moment you seek within yourself

To power through one more day
To power past the madness

And misunderstood, misconstrued, miserable falling
You pick yourself put yourself into context

The world speaks, the world can lie,
those genuine will walk

Will wake through your sorrow and rise
through the dark

Let those people in, forgive, forget,
keep walking layer by layer seeking and revitalizing

The Ventriloquist

A projection of the invalidated heart
a debrief of one's emptiness catapulted
into the nuances of extremities
a silence unheard and a truth unspoken

Beyond the introvert and past the extrovert
Beside the broken and slapped expulsion

A serenity that never was to be
A foresight that never could be
A projection as clear as can be
A white cloth tainted will never be
A scar that hurtfully gleams

Sprinkled ego that blames the weep
Victimized and tormented atrocities
None beyond measured none that reaped
The fault of all responsibility of nobody
The eyes tear is nobody hearing me

Serenade

The symphony of silence crackling through
Eyes meet past the black brim
The blush in your eyes the wit in mine
The tale that moved past
The tale that saw dark

The agony of disproportionate misery
An irony of lies as sincerity is blatantly perpetrated
An advocate of the devil, a pain creamed rationality
As love it seems enables an addiction

Letting go to give in a one lost identity
To search the voice box within, the angelic scream
The subconscious dwells in the darkest alleys
A beautiful melody with a dividend prose

Subtracted lies and substantiated witnesses
A reasoned crime in giving all one has
The melody breezes through blowing off the bruising
The strings sit atop the rhythm of the heartbeat

As the gasps are intermittent
and the thoughts are eclectic

A walk past the concrete and into the shadows

The melody follows an emptiness

that will never be filled

6. Reclusive Recovery

*'**Reclusive Recovery**' is embracing life beyond the cage. As remnants of the past come forth, one also views their patterns of self-sabotage. One realizes how much suffering they are doing and how much isn't. Through learning from others, through learning from themselves, ultimately they find comfort in an intentionally reclusive recovery plan. There is now trust in the inner silence, a reducing dependency to seek for happiness externally. Someday the individual shall get there, today he shall smile. As he smiles, he realizes he is already where he sees himself to be.*

"Unfriend"

All it took was a message
Straightforward, assumed & decided
I perhaps round off the harness
For years to have been
A friend that once was is now never to be

I looked at it. No! It stared at me!
Cold blooded anger, despondency
The stiffness grew stronger, my eyes went weak
3 years did not matter
A friend that once was is now never to be

I asked why but silence grew solemnly
As I sat down chocked and in uncertainty
My memory of recent gave up on me
Our hugs and rejoice now will never be
A friend that once was is now never to be
I wished you had told me
For I felt wrong

For nothing or something what went wrong?
Snivelled in despair I can't speak certainty
A friend that once was is now never to be

Now 5 years later I stand fixated

On what could have been stronger

Yet the reasons fall short

For what never was damaged what was not wronged

A friend that once was is never to be

Authority

"Can I buy this necklace?"
she requested her prince
He said,
"Of course, my love, whatever you want"
Did he? I thought.
Did she? I felt.

"I want to have 3 kids!"
He said to his princess
She said,
"Your wish is my command."
Did he? I stared
Did she? I wondered

I related 30 years later Déjà vu struck a similar chord
"You will do as told"
The king instructed his queen
"Definitely, I'm sorry."
The queen nervously fumbled

Forerunners and flag-bearers of authority
"Mother, please do as we need you to!"
3 young men came running into my shop

The mother looked down at herself,
Wrecked, old, duty-bound she said
"Of course, my love, whatever you want"

10 years further the shop is still same old
Whitebeard and with a hoarse voice I said
"Ma'am, how can I be there for you today?"
The same bride, the same mother long past
She looked at me and she wept

The baggage of a patterned loop
The baggage of a terrified past
The baggage of a replayed future
"That is enough for another 100 years."
She left smiling

For the first time, I saw her a final time before
she closed the doors behind her
she felt liberated and smiled
Her lips were wet with the tears
trickling down her cheek
She held her heart and lipped *"Thank you"*

Authority and liberation are often misconstrued
An allowance perhaps is a better suit

A few hours later my little girl came
running in with her mother
Her mother asked nervously
"Could I enrol our child in a wrestling workshop?"
My daughter looked at me hoping for approval,
subject to my authority

My wife's trembling hands and
my daughter's innocent eyes

Unconsciously, the social construct is an inevitability
First my wife and now my daughter
I left them in fear as I walked towards a mirror
I feared the fear I instilled in my wife and daughter

The fear of authority, allowance, dominance
As I strolled towards the door
The same pained mother walked past
Breathing for the first time
Smiling until the next fright

As my two precious pearls looked at me disturbingly
I approached my wife and held her trembling hands
"You have just as much right as I do, I love you." I said

The 5 minutes of silence was so beautiful
She cried happily, for the freedom I gave her,
was not mine to give
For the allowance I gave was never mine to give
The trembling stopped as her tears wet my shirt
My daughter watching us perplexed
I knelt to my daughter and her mother with my wedding ring and
said
"I promise to take good care of both of you.
You are just as much mine as much I am yours."

My wife's shoulders relaxed off the baggage carried
My daughter was still bewildered as I spoke further
"Child, you may not decipher what I say now but someday you will"
She looked intently
"You are your freedom. You are your own master."
She smiled impressed and relieved

The social construct does not discriminate on age
The baggage of authority
on her fragile shoulders had been lifted
We hugged each other for the first time
All of us were in tears as I took them for an ice cream and said
"Child and wife, whatever you decide to do, I am here for you."
Unconditionally, wholeheartedly and unreservedly

The Quest

Rest assured karma seems indifferent
but is fair as a higher intelligence
For you have done good,
more good and nothing but good

The bad days have long past gone
I heard a screenplay perhaps
already written and rewritten

My soul ripped apart, the breath
I can still feel
A multitude of speeches and help books to read

Nothing that could magically heal the wound
A screenplay perhaps already written and rewritten

There are the so called 'Bad' people
the evil manufactures
My soul ripped apart, the breath I can still feel

While I reassess my life rather poorly
I feel I have failed myself more than ever
This delusion needs to be broken promptly

No self talk or self help helped
My soul ripped apart, the breath I can still feel
Wincing in pain I sucked in the coldness of the air

I looked at the stars, the few on the day
Knew there was no silver lining to guide me
Misery and agony took turns to slice me open

My soul ripped apart, the breath I can still feel
My inner voice lost in the thickness of the aftermath
Expect nothing and you shall be rewarded

For I did no wrong and still paid the price
Misery and agony took turns to slice me open
My soul ripped apart, the breath I can still feel

The sweetness of angelic voices
The thumping of the bass
The long tradition of praying hard
Yet misery and agony took turns

My soul ripped apart, the breath I can still feel
I caved in further wiping the sweat off my palms
Writing my farewell and staring into uncertainty

The symphony of music like never before hit me

The repetition of goodwill and support did its best

My soul ripped apart, the breath I can still feel

I did no wrong and that was my only respite

For I lived by my values

No evidence to disprove that

My soul ripped apart, the breath I can still feel

But I know my truth and I look the devil in the eye

I slowly start picking myself up

From one dark moment within 4 walls

To a series of dark moments in outer space

I know my truth, I stare into the devils eye

I pick myself up again, limping yet trying

I find I rose Like the phoenix bird

In all the moments i Istayed alive

And as I am alive writing this

I hope I'm alive when you read this too

In the truth I know no shame

In all the moments I stayed alive

I lived on for another moment

Reality never ceasing to disappoint
The lost control I grip again
I know my truth and I know no shame

The Last Name

History played on loop
Thoughts exploding as the oceans on mute
I see a fake smile strongly advocating
The truth created by a mind and fostered
From its root.

Deaf ears are a certain weaponry
One can itch A way through to certainty
The truth doesn't matter it's the tone sadly
The cowardly get to a supreme height
enchanting new promises with a cherry top tier

Embracing what is wrong
but masking it airtight.
The striking observation
of this cruelty is that win or lose,
The truth remains a lie

Signature never doubted,
owned by only one
feared upon by his own
yet loved by the crowd respected, sympathized with,
nobody's seen the other side;
up and shiny after sunrise brutal,

cruel in the dark waving proudly

A demeanour will not know the ends
A dimmer hoping it stays within
this era never ever passes on
hoping the end is somewhere near
pray the last name ends its song

Someday

Dried leaves wet a painful road
imprints so dark chills deep down low
shallow dim lights, shivering shore,
joy-filled sorrow lost control.

Every word said pasted in my heart
all the memories are like a broken star
that smothered through my very skin
and down I lie face down sinking

Through the fall
through the dark and
the autumns growth
summer cold restless
hopes steaming from below

Like a cup filled half
and a smile untold
but the clouds seem strong
and the storm behold

As the lies seem firm onto nothingness
all the promises weep and the emptiness

like A paper crumpled like A weeping child
all the comfort brings out the devil inside

Someday it will end someday
you will smile holding hands
and words that will comfort your try
someday it will end
someday you will smile

Feed that hope inside you
that help will fix you alive
someday it will end
someday you will smile

I will hold you strong
you will fly again high
someday it will end

Someday you will smile
that someday is today
'cause that feeling inside

Pluck your heart from the dark
wash it with your might
families, friends you've got an army right
let the words flow

don't give your sight away

someday it will end today you shall smile

www.ingramcontent.com/pod-product-compliance
Lightning Source LLC
Chambersburg PA
CBHW022031150726
47990CB00002B/918